The Money Multiplier

Growing Your Wealth Through Smart Investment

Andrew Galowey

Copyright © [Andrew Galowey] [2024]. All rights reserved. No part of this publication may be reproduced, distributed, or transmitted in any form or by any means, including photocopying, recording, or other electronic or mechanical methods, without the prior written permission of the publisher, except in the case of brief quotations embodied in critical reviews and certain other noncommercial uses permitted by copyright law.

Table Of Contents

Introduction

Chapter 1: Planting the Seed: Understanding Your Financial Goals and Risk Tolerance

Chapter 2: From Acorn to Oak: Creating the Foundation for Your Investment Portfolio

Chapter 3: Cultivating Knowledge: Key Investment Vehicles and Strategies

Chapter 4: Weathering the Storms: Risk Management and Portfolio Optimization

Chapter 5: Harvesting the Rewards: Long-term Strategies and Retirement Planning

Conclusion

Introduction

Have you ever desired financial freedom? Of witnessing your money rise slowly, thanks to the power of clever investing? In "The Money Multiplier: Growing Your Wealth Through Smart Investment," we'll go on this adventure together.

This book is not a compilation of get-rich-quick methods. It's a road plan for accumulating long-term wealth via prudent and knowledgeable investing techniques. We'll start by building the framework, helping you identify your financial objectives and risk tolerance. Then we'll go into the principles of constructing a diverse portfolio, investigating alternative investing vehicles, and navigating the ever-changing market environment.

Whether you're a total novice or wanting to improve your current investing strategy, "The Money Multiplier" will provide you with the information and skills you need to nurture financial stability and enjoy the benefits of your carefully planned investments. Are you prepared to change your financial future? Let's get started.

Chapter 1: Planting the Seed: Understanding Your Financial Goals and Risk Tolerance

Have you ever looked at a huge oak tree, its branches reaching for the sky, and felt its quiet strength? Little did you know, that huge monster started as a little acorn, carefully nourished in healthy soil. Creating money via investing follows a similar process. Just as a healthy oak takes meticulous preparation before blossoming, establishing financial stability necessitates a clear grasp of your objectives and a prudent attitude to risk. This chapter is the fertile field where we sow the seeds for your investing journey.

The Power of Goals:

Imagine setting sail on a vast ocean without a destination in mind. You could float aimlessly, swept by the winds of doubt. Similarly, investing without a stated aim is a formula for failure. Start by determining your financial ambitions. Do you desire for a pleasant retirement? Perhaps you dream of establishing a company, supporting your child's education, or going on a lavish globe vacation. Write out these objectives, be explicit about deadlines and target amounts.

Visualizing these objectives has a twofold function. First, it gives a strong incentive to remain committed to your investing strategy. When confronted with short-term temptations, your long-term objectives will act as a guiding light, reminding you of the greater picture. Second, well stated objectives help you to establish a focused investing approach. The timescale for your objective plays a vital impact — shorter-term ambitions could necessitate a more cautious strategy, while long-term aims allow for higher risk tolerance.

Identifying Your Risk Tolerance:

Investing necessarily includes risk. The stock market swings, firms go bankrupt, and unexpected economic events might have an influence on your money. However, risk is not a monster to be feared, but rather a force that must be recognized and handled. Your risk tolerance refers to your degree of comfort with probable losses. Are you someone who sleeps well even when the market falls? Or do you lose sleep with every economic slump headline?

There are several factors to consider when determining your risk tolerance. Age plays a role. In general, younger investors have a longer investing horizon and can bear more risk. Their investments have greater time to recover from market volatility. Financial stability also influences risk tolerance. Individuals with a sufficient emergency fund and little debt may afford to take greater risks in their investing portfolio. Personality also has a role. Some people are innately risk-averse, whilst others thrive on a calculated gamble.

Risk tolerance is not a set value. It can change over time, influenced by life experiences and shifting financial circumstances. However, being aware of your current risk tolerance is critical for making sound investment decisions.

Risk Tolerance and Investment Options:

Understanding your risk tolerance can help you choose proper investment instruments. Stocks often provide large potential rewards but also substantial risk. Bonds are often regarded less risky but give lower yields. Mutual funds and ETFs provide diversity, but their risk levels vary based on the underlying assets.

Let's provide an example. Imagine Alex, a 25-year-old recent graduate. Sarah has a secure employment and low debt. She has a lengthy investing horizon for her retirement plans. Alexes minimal financial responsibilities and extended timeframe suggest that she can accept a greater risk portfolio, which may include a bigger allocation to equities. On the other hand, David, a 55-year-old approaching retirement, has different objectives. David must safeguard capital and provide a consistent revenue source. His portfolio will most likely trend more strongly toward bonds and other low-risk assets.

Investing is a journey, not a destination. Understanding your objectives and accepting your risk tolerance are the first steps in laying the groundwork for your financial future. These core aspects will serve as the guiding principles for establishing a diversified portfolio and navigating the ever-changing investing environment. In the following chapters, we will explore further into numerous investment vehicles, methods, and tactics, all with the goal of enabling you to build long-term wealth and accomplish your financial objectives. Remember that, just as a big oak grows from a little acorn, your financial journey begins with a single, well-defined seed.

Chapter 2: From Acorn to Oak: Creating the Foundation for Your Investment Portfolio

In Chapter 1, we discussed the necessity of establishing your financial objectives and risk tolerance before embarking on your investing path. Now it's time to cultivate that seed and see it develop into a strong oak - your investment portfolio. This chapter will provide you with the information required to build a solid basis for long-term wealth growth.

The Power of Diversification:

Imagine putting all your eggs in one basket. If you drop that basket, all the eggs will shatter. The same idea applies to investment. Putting all of your money in one investment exposes you to severe danger. A firm might go bankrupt, an industry can suffer a slump, or an unanticipated economic catastrophe can devastate a certain asset class. Diversification is the foundation of an effective investing plan. It entails diversifying your assets across asset types, which reduces risk.

There are various methods to diversify. Asset allocation is the division of your portfolio into various asset classes. The most frequent breakdown consists of:

- Stocks represent ownership in a company and have the potential for high returns, but they also carry a higher risk due to market volatility.

- Bonds are loans given to businesses or governments that provide a consistent revenue stream while posing less risk than equities.

- Cash and cash equivalents include savings accounts, money market funds, and certificates of deposit. They provide minimal risk but lesser rewards.

Your risk tolerance and investing objectives will determine the best asset allocation for you. A younger investor with a longer time horizon may allocate more to equities for future growth, while someone approaching retirement may prefer bonds for income and capital preservation.

Beyond the Basics: Exploring Alternative Investments

WhileG stocks, bonds, and cash equivalents are the foundation of most portfolios, there are several alternative assets to consider. These may help diversify your portfolio and may provide uncorrelated returns, which means their performance is not directly related to the stock market. Examples include:

- Real estate investments, whether direct or via Real Estate Investment Trusts (REITs), may provide rental

income as well as possible value increase.
- Commodities include precious metals like gold, agricultural items like wheat, and energy sources such as oil. They may offer a buffer against inflation, although they are often volatile.
- Collectibles: Art, antiques, and rare coins may rise in value over time, but the market might be illiquid, meaning it could be difficult to sell them fast.

Remember, alternative investments sometimes involve greater risks and need specialized understanding. Do your due investigation before going into these asset groups.

Building Your Investment Arsenal: Popular Investment Vehicles

Now that you understand the value of .diversity, let's look at several common investment vehicles that might help you develop your portfolio:

- Individual Stocks: Owning stock in certain firms has the potential for big gains, but it also includes substantial risk due to the company's performance.
- Mutual Funds: Pool your money with other investors to invest in a portfolio of assets overseen by a professional fund manager. They provide versatility and convenience, but there are costs.

- Exchange-Traded Funds (ETFs) are similar to mutual funds, except they trade on stock exchanges alongside individual equities. They have cheaper costs and better transparency than certain mutual funds.

- Index Funds: Passively monitor a market index, such the S&P 500, delivering wide diversification and minimal costs.

- These are just a few examples; the best combination for you depends on your objectives and risk tolerance.

Building a solid basis for your financial portfolio entails diversifying and selecting the appropriate investment vehicles. Remember, asset allocation is critical, and there is no one-size-fits-all solution. Before making any selections, consider your risk tolerance and do research into various asset classes and investing possibilities. The chapters that follow will go into further detail about various investing strategies and practices that will assist you in growing your financial oak tree and seeing your money accumulate over time.

Chapter 3: Cultivating Knowledge: Key Investment Vehicles and Strategies

In prior chapters, we established the foundation for your investing path. You've set your financial objectives, evaluated your risk tolerance, and understood the need of diversity in developing a good portfolio. Now it's time to go deeper and discover the most important tools and methods at your disposal. This chapter will teach you how to develop a healthy investment garden.

Understand Your Investment Options:

We investigated numerous investment vehicles in Chapter 2, but let's take a deeper look at several significant possibilities and their distinguishing features:

- Stocks: Representing ownership in a corporation, stocks have the potential for considerable wealth gain but also pose significant risk. Stock prices may be influenced by several factors such as corporate performance, industry developments, and market circumstances. It is critical to do research on particular firms before making an investment.

- Mutual Funds: These professionally managed investment pools provide both diversity and convenience. Mutual funds invest in a variety of assets, including stocks, bonds, and a mix of both. They exist in a variety of types, each concentrating on a certain industry, development potential, or revenue generating. Mutual funds often impose fees, which might reduce your returns.

- Exchange-Traded Funds (ETFs): Like mutual funds, ETFs follow a certain index or investing strategy. However, unlike mutual funds, ETFs trade on stock markets every day, providing more flexibility and possibly cheaper expenses. When selecting an ETF, consider its cost ratio (annual management charge) and underlying holdings.

Index funds are a sort of exchange-traded fund or mutual fund that passively follows a market index. They provide extensive diversity at modest fees. Because they seek to duplicate index performance, they often provide steady, if modest, returns.

Investment Strategy for Growth and Income

Beyond selecting the appropriate investment vehicles, there are tactics you may use to manage your portfolio and possibly increase returns:

- Dollar-Cost Averaging (DCA) entails investing a certain amount of money at regular periods, regardless of asset price. This strategy averages the cost per share across time, reducing the influence of market changes. DCA is an effective method for long-term investors that follow a disciplined approach.

- Asset Rebalancing: As various asset classes perform differently, your portfolio allocation will deviate from your target percentages. Rebalancing entails selling outperforming assets and purchasing underperforming ones to restore your desired asset allocation. This helps you retain your risk tolerance while also diversifying your portfolio.

- Tax-Advantaged Accounts: Using tax-advantaged accounts such as IRAs and 401(k)s may dramatically increase your investment returns. Contributions to these accounts may be tax deductible, and gains are frequently tax-deferred until withdrawn in retirement.

Additional considerations:

- Fees: Investment vehicles often include fees, such as expense ratios for mutual funds and ETFs or charges for stock transactions. Be careful of these costs and choose solutions that are consistent with your investing objectives and budget.

- Dividend Reinvestment: Many stocks and mutual funds pay dividends, which are a percentage of a company's income given to its owners. Consider reinvesting these dividends to increase your earnings over time.

- Staying informed: The financial world is continuously changing. Stay current on economic trends, market movements, and corporate news that may affect your investments.

Remember, this is simply an overview of several important investing vehicles and methods. Conduct your own research, speak with a financial professional if necessary, and choose solutions that are consistent with your risk tolerance and financial objectives.

Growing a successful investment garden takes expertise and continual maintenance. This chapter has given you the necessary skills to explore the world of investing opportunities and strategies. Remember that consistency, dedication, and a long-term mindset are essential components for success. In the next chapters, we will look at risk management tactics as well as strategies for long-term wealth growth and retirement planning. With devotion and the information gained from this book, you may see your investment garden grow and enjoy the benefits of your financial efforts.

Chapter 4: Weathering the Storms: Risk Management and Portfolio Optimization

The investing path, like life itself, is not without its challenges. Market volatility, unexpected economic events, and even personal situations might cause turbulence in your portfolio. However, much as a strong oak weathers storms, a well-managed portfolio may overcome these obstacles. This chapter provides you with the resources you need to properly manage risk and improve your portfolio for long-term success.

Understanding risk management

Risk management is not about removing all risk from your assets. Instead, it's about limiting its effects and safeguarding your assets. Here are some important methods to consider:

- diversity: As previously said, diversity remains the foundation of risk management. Spreading your assets across many asset classes helps to mitigate the impact of a downturn in any one industry.

- Asset Allocation: Maintaining your intended asset allocation via rebalancing is critical. When markets move, your portfolio percentages may vary. Rebalancing entails purchasing underperforming assets while selling outperforming ones in order to restore your desired risk profile.

- Stop-Loss Orders: These are instructions to your broker that will automatically sell a security if its price falls below a specified threshold. This helps reduce possible losses in a turbulent market, but it may also result in lost chances if the price recovers swiftly.

Dollar-Cost Averaging (DCA), as mentioned in Chapter 3, is a risk-management method on its own. By spending a certain amount at regular times, you may average out the cost per share over time, lessening the influence of market volatility on your total investment cost.

Beyond the Basics: Advanced Risk Management Techniques

For more sophisticated investors, further risk management measures might be employed.

Options trading: Options contracts provide the right, but not the responsibility, to purchase or sell a securities at a certain price by a given date. They may be used to protect current holdings, reduce losses, or produce revenue. Options trading requires a thorough grasp of the market and involves substantial risk.

Short selling is the practice of borrowing shares of a company that you predict will fall in price, selling them immediately, and then repurchasing them at a reduced price to repay the lender. Short selling is a high-risk technique that should only be used by experienced investors.

Hedging is utilizing several financial instruments to offset probable losses in another investment. For example, an investor who owns equities may also buy put options on those stocks, which would yield a return if the stock price fell. Hedging methods may be complicated and need careful study.

Portfolio optimization

Once you've mastered risk management, you may explore portfolio optimization approaches. The idea here is to maximize your predicted return given a certain degree of risk tolerance. Here are some things to consider:

- Modern Portfolio Theory (MPT) proposes that investors may create optimum portfolios by taking into account not just individual asset returns, but also their relationships. Assets with low correlations may assist to lower overall portfolio risk.

- Efficient Frontier: This notion refers to the set of optimum portfolios that provide the maximum anticipated return for a given amount of risk. Investors may choose a portfolio from the efficient frontier that matches their risk tolerance.

- Risk-Adjusted Performance Measures: Metrics such as the Sharpe Ratio and Sortino Ratio take into account the risk required to attain such results. These might help you assess the success of your portfolio and compare it to other assets.

Remember that advanced risk management approaches and portfolio optimization might be complicated. If you are thinking about incorporating these methods into your portfolio, talk to a financial professional first.

Market storms are unavoidable, but with smart risk management and an emphasis on optimization, your portfolio can weather them and stay on course for long-term success. This chapter's techniques will provide you the skills you need to confidently navigate the financial world. Remember that a well-diversified portfolio, rigorous rebalancing, and a long-term outlook are critical components of a robust investing approach. The next chapter will look at long-term wealth growth and solutions for retirement planning.

Chapter 5: Harvesting the Rewards: Long-term Strategies and Retirement Planning

The seeds you sowed in Chapter 1 have grown into a successful investment garden. You've handled market volatility and positioned your portfolio for growth. Now it's time to reap the benefits of your long-term investing adventure. This chapter discusses wealth building tactics and effective retirement planning.

The Power of Time and Compound Interest

Albert Einstein famously referred to compound interest as the "eighth wonder of the world." Simply put, it is the interest gained on your interest. Over time, the power of compounding may considerably increase your wealth. Let's use an example:

Assume Alex begins investing $1,000 each year at the age of 25, with an anticipated return of 7%. If she continues to make these payments until she reaches the age of 65 and never withdraws any cash, her total investment will be $62,142. However, compound interest may increase the total value of her portfolio at retirement to an astonishing $340,138.

This example demonstrates the value of getting started early and allowing your assets to expand over time. The sooner you begin, the longer compound interest has to work its magic.

Creating a Retirement Nest Egg:

Retirement planning requires a dedicated strategy. Here are some important methods to consider:

- Calculate Your Retirement Needs: Determine your ideal retirement lifestyle and the yearly income required to sustain it. Consider inflation, healthcare expenditures, and prospective trip plans.

- Maximize Employer-Sponsored Plans: Many workplaces provide retirement plans, such as 401(k), with employer matching contributions. Take full use of these programs to speed up your money building.

- Contribute to an IRA: Individual Retirement Accounts (IRAs) provide tax benefits for retirement savings. Traditional IRAs accept tax-deductible contributions, but Roth IRAs provide tax-free withdrawals in retirement. Choose the one that best fits your tax situation.

- Increase Investment Contributions: As your income rises, aim to increase your investment contributions.

Consider setting up automatic transfers to guarantee that you consistently save and invest for retirement.

Investment Strategies for Retirement:

While your general risk tolerance remains an important consideration, your retirement investing plan may change as you approach your goal date. Here are some considerations.

- Asset Allocation for Retirement: As you approach retirement, you may want to gradually change your portfolio to more conservative assets, such as bonds, to decrease risk and safeguard your collected cash.

- Target-Date Funds are a straightforward way to prepare for retirement. Target-date funds automatically change their asset allocation over time, becoming more conservative as the retirement date approaches.

- Income-Producing Investments: Including dividend-paying stocks and bonds in your portfolio may offer a consistent source of income in retirement.

Beyond the Numbers: Planning for a Successful Retirement:

Retirement is about more than just financial stability. Consider these factors while preparing for the future:

- Lifestyle Planning: Do you want to explore the globe, spend time with family, or pursue hobbies? Incorporate these goals into your retirement planning.

- Healthcare Expenses: Healthcare costs might be high in retirement. Investigate possible healthcare requirements and include health insurance expenses into your retirement budget.

Location: Where would you want to retire? Living expenses might vary greatly based on region. Consider this while calculating your necessary retirement income.

Harvesting the benefits of your investing journey requires a long-term mindset and a focus on both financial stability and personal joy. You may build a comfortable nest egg for your elderly years by emphasizing continuous savings, using tax-advantaged accounts, and implementing proper investment methods. Remember that planning goes beyond cash; picturing your ideal lifestyle and healthcare requirements enables a well-rounded retirement plan. With devotion, the seeds you sow now will grow into a future of financial stability and the opportunity to follow your interests in retirement.

Conclusion

This book has provided you with the information and skills you need to navigate the investing environment, manage risk, and build a successful investment portfolio. Remember that generating money is a marathon, not a sprint. Maintain your commitment to your long-term objectives, be disciplined in your investing strategy, and always seek fresh information.

The financial world is always changing, but the essential ideas discussed in this book remain consistent. You can alter your financial destiny and accomplish your goals by embracing diversity, managing risk properly, and taking advantage of compound interest. Let your investing adventure begin; the seeds of wealth are ready to be sown!

www.ingramcontent.com/pod-product-compliance
Lightning Source LLC
Chambersburg PA
CBHW050250230526
45470CB00005B/2202